About the maps

The guide features maps showing the various sections of the Hidden Highway, and a sample of one is shown on the right, together with the key. They are sufficiently detailed for navigation – but you may wish to supplement them with more detailed maps.

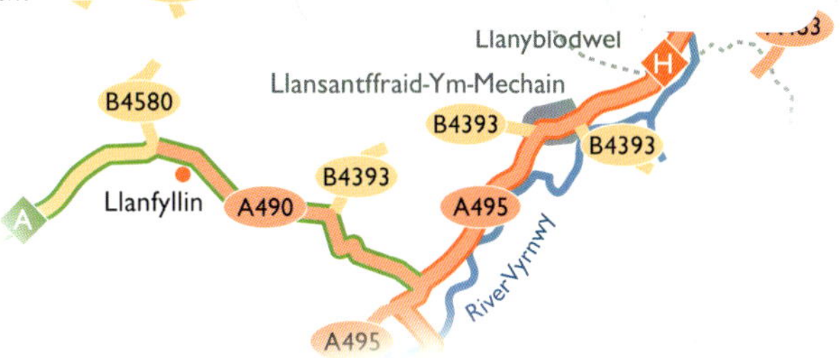

Staying overnight

If you are planning to travel all of the Hidden Highway, you will probably want to stay the night somewhere en route. There are many wonderful places to stay near the Hidden Highway. Any of the Tourist Information Centres below will be able to find a room that's right for you in their area.

Shropshire

Mile End, **Oswestry** SY11 4JA
Tel. 01691 662488;
Fax 01691 662883

The Music Hall, The Square, **Shrewsbury** SY1 1LH
Tel. 01743 281200;
Fax 01743 281213

Castle Street, **Ludlow** SY8 1AS
Tel. 01584 875053;
Fax 01584 877931

Herefordshire

1 King Street, **Hereford** HR4 9BW
Tel. 01432 268430;
Fax 01432 342662

Swan House, Edde Cross Street, **Ross-on-Wye** HR9 7BZ
Tel. 01989 562768;
Fax 01989 565057

3 The Homend, **Ledbury** HR8 1BN
Tel. 01531 636147;
Fax 01531 634313

Wales

The Shire Hall, Broad Street, **Presteigne**, Powys LD8 2AW
Tel. 01544 260650

Old Town Hall, Memorial Gardens, **Llandrindod Wells**, Powys LD1 5DL
Tel. 01597 822600

The Vicarage Gardens Car Park, Church Street, **Welshpool**, Powys SY21 7DD
Tel. 01938 552043

Cheshire

Chester Visitor Centre, Vicar's Lane, **Chester** CH1 1XQ
Tel. 01244 402111

For advance bookings, visit:
www.visitorlinks.com

Bookable website:
www.mid-wales-tourism.org.uk

Freephone booking service:
0800 27 37 47;
from outside UK, dial +44 1654 703526

For further information on the Hidden Highway, visit:
www.hidden-highway.com

Opposite: Ludlow

For further information on Herefordshire, Shropshire and Mid Wales:

Herefordshire Tourism,
Herefordshire Council, PO Box 44,
Leominster HR6 8ZD
Tel. 01432 260621; Fax 01432 260620;
email tourism@herefordshire.gov.uk

Shropshire Tourism,
Unit 13, Harlescott Barns, Harlescott,
Shrewsbury SY1 3SZ
Tel. 01743 462462; Fax 01743 462035;
email shropshire.tourism@virgin.net

Mid Wales Tourism,
The Station, Machynlleth,
Powys SY20 8TG
Tel. 01654 702653; Fax 01654 703235
Website with bookings facility:
www.mid-wales-tourism.org.uk

Key to the maps

Minor road (not numbered)
B4220 Minor road
A449 Major road
H Hidden Highway (following minor road)
A Hidden Highway alternative (following major road)
T Hidden Highway 'time to spare' (following un-numbered road)
Eastnor ● Place of interest
Built up area
River
Wales/England border
Railway
NT National Trust
EH English Heritage

Other routes along the way

Cider Route: Ross-on-Wye, Ledbury, Hereford

Brother Cadfael Car Trails: Ludlow, Craven Arms, Shrewsbury, Oswestry

King Arthur's Trail: Shrewsbury, Welshpool, Oswestry

Ghostly Shropshire Car Trails: Shrewsbury

Housman Trail: Ludlow, Craven Arms, Clun

Black and White Village Trail: Leominster, Kington

These trails are available from the relevant Tourist Information Centres or tourism departments

Research and concept by Fielder Green Associates and Lesley Davies Associates.

Photography by Neil Jinkerson, John Brooks, Andrew Perkins and Eric West of Jarrold Publishing, Archie Miles, Bill Meadows, Wales Tourist Board, Herefordshire Council, Mike Hayward, Robert Eames, Gareth Thomas, Gordon Dickins, Shropshire Tourism, Cordelia Weedon, Kevin J. Richardson, Mid Wales Tourism, Oswestry and Welsh Border Tourist Association and Oswestry Borough Council.

Design and mapping by Kaarin Wall.

ISBN 0-7117-1511-4

Designed and produced by Jarrold Publishing, Norwich.
Printed in Great Britain 1/00
www.jarrold-publishing.co.uk

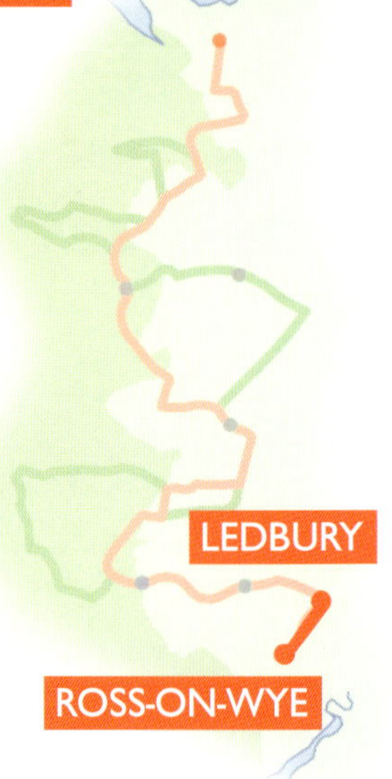

Ross-on-Wye

An attractive town in the heart of the Wye Valley, Ross is set high on a sandstone cliff overlooking the river. Timbered houses cluster around a seventeenth-century market whose first charter was granted by King Stephen in 1138. However trade had been carried out here long before that, and was so important to the town that the streets were laid out deliberately to create the triangular market place. Markets are held on Thursdays and Saturdays and the Market House is home to the Ross-on-Wye Heritage Trust.

Opposite the market is the house of the local philanthropist John Kyrle (1637–1724). He did much to beautify the town and its surroundings, gave it its first water supply, founded schools and charities, and set up a dispensary to give medicines to the poor. Kyrle was immortalised as 'The Man of Ross' in a poem by Alexander Pope and even donated a bell to **St Mary's**, the town's parish church. Founded in 1284, much of it had to be rebuilt after it was struck by lightning in 1852.

Ross hosts an **International Festival of Music and Dance** each year, held during the last two weeks of August.

The town is at the heart of the Wye Valley Area of Outstanding Natural Beauty. Probably the best way of exploring this is via the long-distance **Wye Valley Walk**, 112 miles (180km), which follows the river from its source at Rhayader to Chepstow, where it joins with the Severn.

To the north of Ross is **Much Marcle**. Its main claim to fame is reflected by the name of a nearby pub – The Slip Tavern – whose sign shows a landslide that occurred in 1575. The area around Ledbury and Much Marcle is known as Big Apple Country, not because of an association with New York but because it is a district famous for its cider. You can take a guided tour of **Weston's Cider** and sample their range of ciders and perries, given unique character by being matured in oak vats. There are also many smaller producers, while the **Big Apple Festival** celebrates apples and cider for two days in May (apple blossom time) and two days in October (when the fruit is harvested).

Ledbury

The ancient market town nestles at the foot of the Malvern Hills, its innumerable old buildings making it a favourite with film producers seeking a location for period drama. The seventeenth-century Market House dominates the town centre and the cobbled Church Lane attracts many photographers.

Top: Market at Ross-on-Wye
Left: The River Wye at Ross

The beautiful Norman parish church, dedicated to **St Michael and All Angels**, has holes in its door made by musket shot during the Battle of Ledbury in 1645. **Butchers' Row House Museum** (an interesting folk museum) is on Church Lane as is the **Heritage Centre** and **Painted Room** where you can examine the unique sixteenth-century frescoes.

The town hosts an annual **Poetry Festival** in June/July, which is a celebration of the best poetry in Britain.

Poetry connections include John Masefield, who was born here; Elizabeth Barrett Browning, who grew up at Hope End, near Ledbury; and the nearby village of Dymock. The latter was famous for its community of poets just before the First World War.

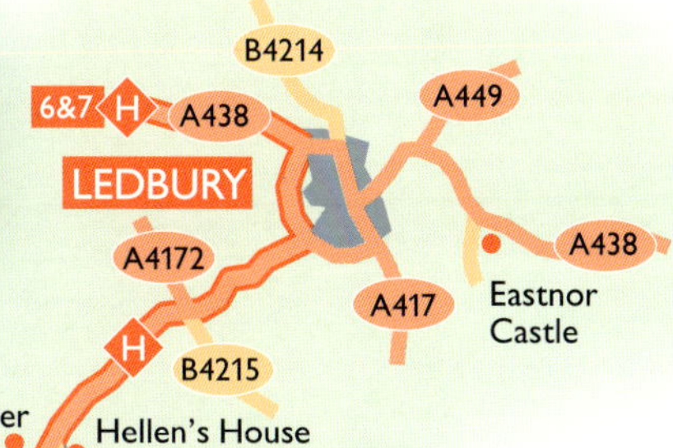

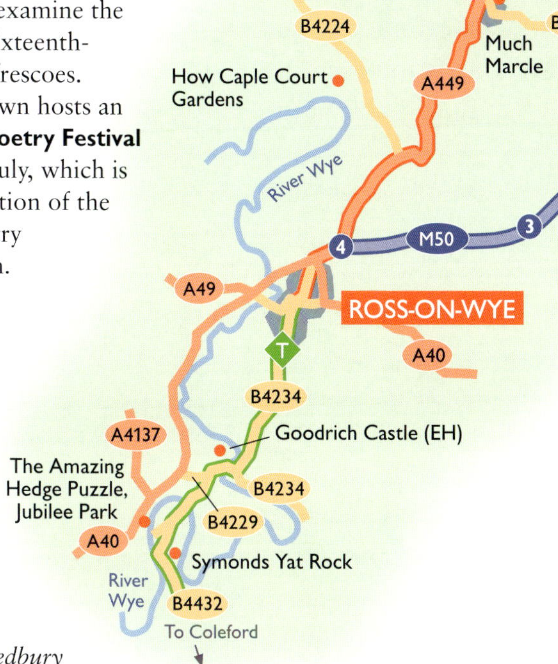

TIME TO SPARE?

The walk to **Symonds Yat Rock** offers spectacular views of the meandering River Wye and the chance to see peregrine falcons. Boat trips on the Wye give different perspectives and are available nearby. Part of the film *Shadowlands*, about Narnia author C.S. Lewis, was filmed here.

Goodrich Castle is a castle of red sandstone with a twelfth-century keep and surrounding towers and walls of a later date. It is the best preserved of all Herefordshire's castles and has a spectacular setting above the Wye.

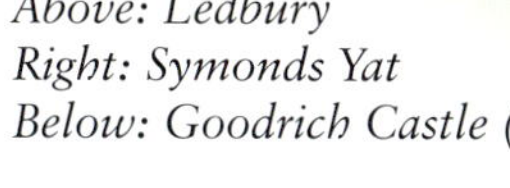

Above: Ledbury
Right: Symonds Yat
Below: Goodrich Castle (EH)

HEREFORD

LEDBURY

Hereford

The ancient cathedral city of Hereford straddles the River Wye at the heart of the lush borderland dividing England and Wales. It is the market centre for an agricultural district famous for its white-faced cattle, cider and hops. Wild salmon from the Wye are also much prized. During the Civil War the city was a Royalist stronghold which twice fell to Parliamentary forces.

The superb **Cathedral**, built of red sandstone, dates from the eleventh century. It houses the **Mappa Mundi** and **Chained Library Exhibition**. The Mappa Mundi is the map of the world drawn around 1290 which gives many fascinating insights into the medieval view of the order of things. The cathedral also has the shrine of St Thomas of Hereford, who was canonised in 1320. It is one of the best-preserved medieval shrines in England.

River Cruises are a relaxing way of viewing the city, or you can take a guided walking tour – both are available in peak season.

Herefordshire produces most of this country's cider. **The Cider Route** begins in

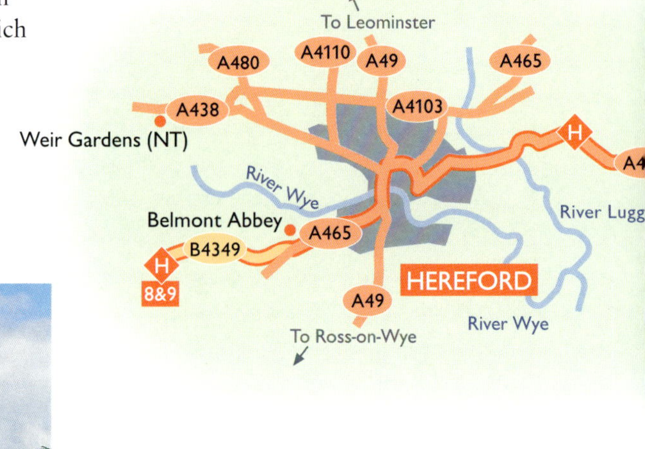

Below: Eastnor Castle, near Ledbury, is a fairytale Georgian castle overlooking a lake with the Malvern Hills as a backdrop. It is surrounded by a deer park.

Hereford and is a voyage of discovery into cider production, embracing eight producers in all, including the world leader, Bulmer's of Hereford, which has a **Visitor Centre**. The start of the route is at the **Cider Museum** and **King Offa's Distillery** where the history of cider production is explained.The story is told that many farm workers around here were paid one-fifth of their wages in cider. Two-gallon a day men were not uncommon!

The **Old House Museum** is at the centre of the city. It was built in 1621 and the furniture dates from this time. **The Waterworks Museum** has massive Victorian pumping engines which help to bring a century of industrial heritage to life in a picturesque riverside setting.

Several famous figures are associated with Hereford. Nell Gwynne, actress and mistress of Charles II, was born in a hovel in what is now Gwynne Street. Edward Elgar lived at Plas Gwyn in Hampton Park Road between 1904 and 1911 and composed two symphonies there.

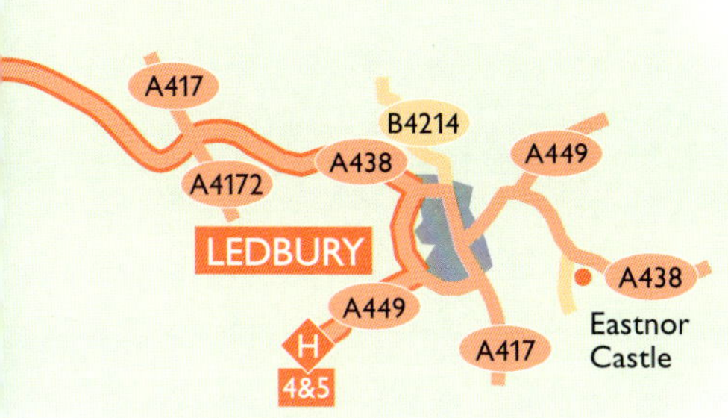

Facing page top: Mappa Mundi

Top: The Cider Museum

Above: The Old Bridge over the River Wye, Hereford

Left: The Chained Library

Centre: Ledbury

Detour at Dorstone up a narrow and winding lane to take in **Arthur's Stone**, an impressive prehistoric burial site cared for by English Heritage. The hilltop gives wide views over beautiful countryside.

Above: Belmont Abbey
Below: Arthur's Stone (EH)

Belmont Abbey, which houses a working community of Benedictine monks, was built in the 1850s and holds a relic of St Thomas of Hereford. Monks guide visitors around the abbey and the surrounding gardens are a haven of peace and tranquillity.

The Golden Valley

The dozen rich and peaceful miles between Hay-on-Wye and Vowchurch seem well named when the sun is low in the sky and drenches the softly folded hills in mellow light. The views are extensive, with the Black Mountains and Brecon Beacons providing distant backdrops. The Golden Valley is mentioned in the film *Shadowlands*, a poignant love story in which Sir Anthony Hopkins played the author C.S. Lewis who wrote the famous Narnia books.

Rather prosaically the name probably came from an old confusion between the Welsh word for water (*dwr*) and the French *d'or*, meaning 'golden'. Romantics like to think that it comes from the legend of a fish wearing a golden chain that was once caught in the river – details of this tale can be found in the parish church at Peterchurch, a building also worth seeing for its architecture.

Vowchurch huddles around its church and has a picturesque setting by the River Dore. Its literary connection is that the brother of Lewis Carroll, author of *Alice in Wonderland*, was the vicar and Carroll often visited the village. Note the fine half-timbered manor house behind the church.

Hay-on-Wye

Hay-on-Wye stands in Wales but its northern and eastern sides border England. The town is world famous for its thirty or so bookshops, a trade begun about fifty years ago by Richard Booth who began by turning a disused cinema into a secondhand bookshop. Bookworms from all corners visit the town each year to browse through a million books; antique dealers and art galleries have also been attracted to premises in its narrow streets. Hay hosts an annual Festival of Literature in early summer which sponsors concerts, readings and other events and is attended by authors and publishers.

The castle stands above the town, often seen as a romantic silhouette on the skyline. It dates from the early thirteenth century and is supposed to be haunted by the wife of its founder, William de Breos.

Two famous long-distance footpaths pass through Hay-on-Wye and both are worth exploring. **The Wye Valley Walk** and **Offa's Dyke Path** give spectacular views within a short distance of the town.

Above: Open-air browsing at Hay-on-Wye

Right: Dore Abbey

Below: Hay-on-Wye

Bottom: Country lane in the Golden Valley

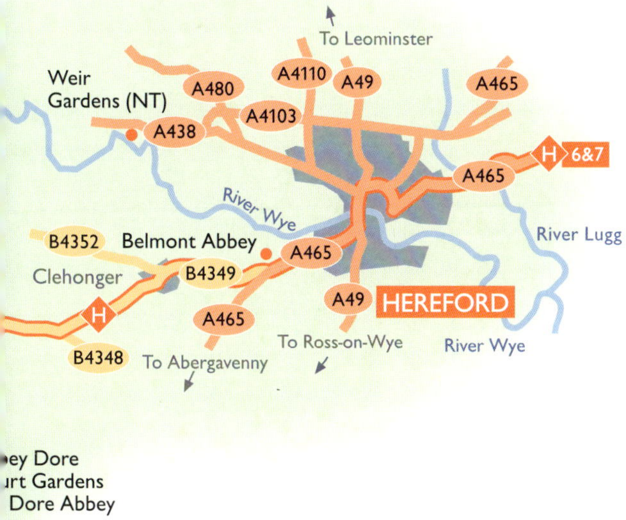

TIME TO SPARE?

At the picturesque hamlet of Abbey Dore you can visit **Dore Abbey**, founded in 1147 by French monks and used as the parish church today. **Abbey Dore Court Gardens** have a unique mix of wild and formal gardens covering six acres (2.4ha).

To Leominster
Weir Gardens (NT)
A480
A4110
A49
A465
A438
A4103
6&7
River Wye
B4352
Belmont Abbey
A465
River Lugg
Clehonger
B4349
A49
HEREFORD
A465
B4348
To Abergavenny
To Ross-on-Wye
River Wye
ey Dore
rt Gardens
Dore Abbey

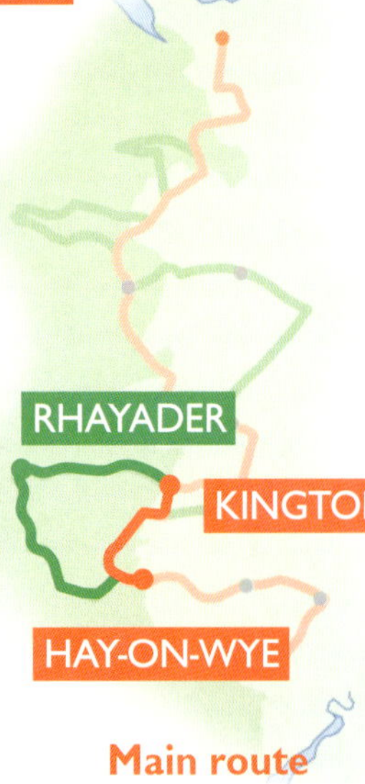

RHAYADER
KINGTON
HAY-ON-WYE
Pen-y-Garreg Reservoir
Garreg-Ddu Reservoir
Claerwen Reservoir
Caban Coch Reservoir
Elan Valley Visitor Centre
A470
B4518
Welsh Royal Crystal
A44
A48
River Wye
A4081
Llandrindod Wells
Newbridge-on-Wye
River Ithon
A470
A483
Royal Welsh Showground
A481
A483
Builth Wells
A470
Aberedw
B4567
A470
Erwood
A47
To Brecon

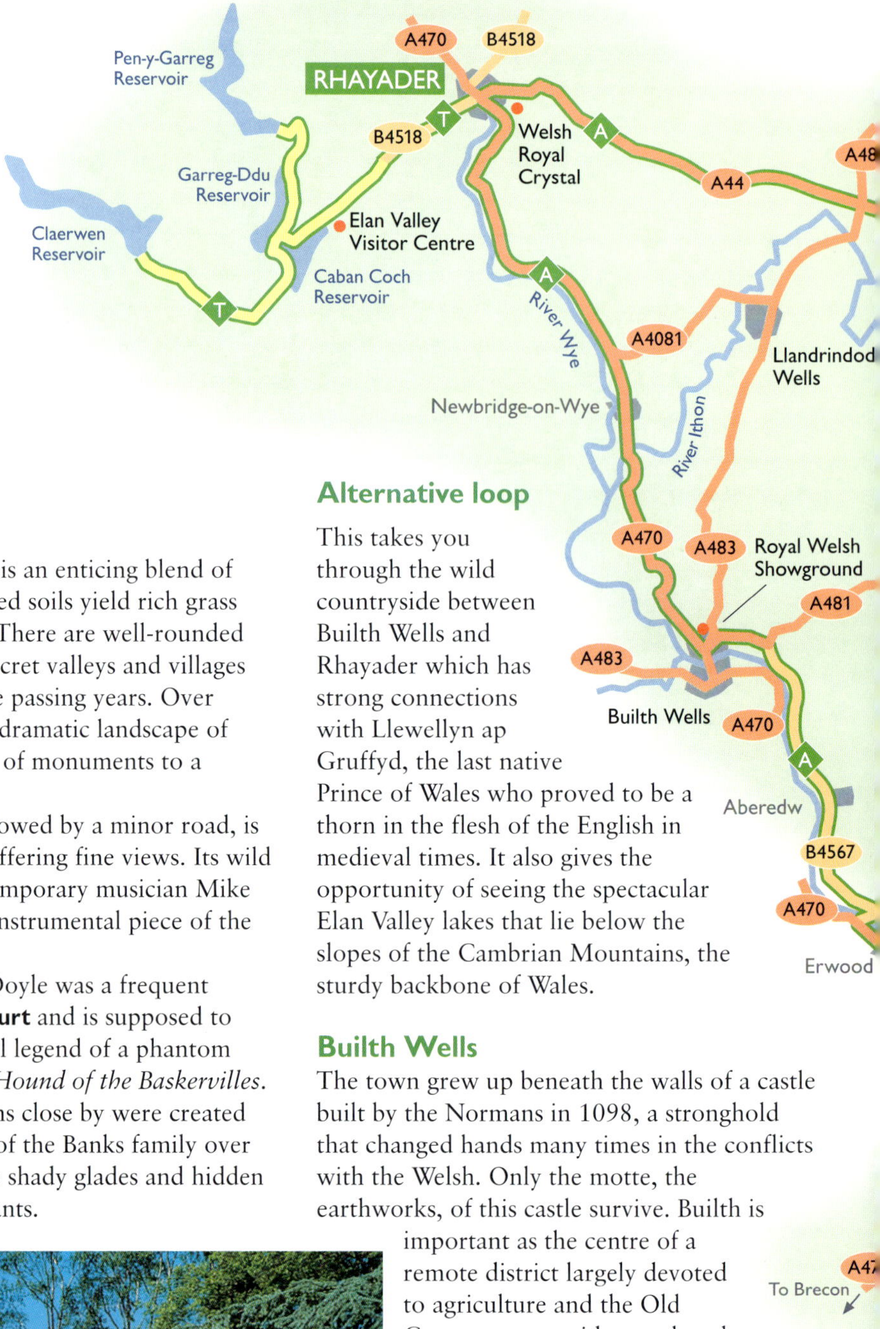

Main route

North Herefordshire is an enticing blend of farmland where the red soils yield rich grass and abundant crops. There are well-rounded hills which conceal secret valleys and villages hardly touched by the passing years. Over the border, the more dramatic landscape of Mid Wales has a host of monuments to a turbulent past.

Hergest Ridge, followed by a minor road, is a geological feature offering fine views. Its wild beauty inspired contemporary musician Mike Oldfield to write an instrumental piece of the same name.

Sir Arthur Conan Doyle was a frequent visitor to **Hergest Court** and is supposed to have borrowed a local legend of a phantom hound to create *The Hound of the Baskervilles.* Hergest Croft Gardens close by were created by three generations of the Banks family over 100 years and feature shady glades and hidden valleys full of rare plants.

Alternative loop

This takes you through the wild countryside between Builth Wells and Rhayader which has strong connections with Llewellyn ap Gruffyd, the last native Prince of Wales who proved to be a thorn in the flesh of the English in medieval times. It also gives the opportunity of seeing the spectacular Elan Valley lakes that lie below the slopes of the Cambrian Mountains, the sturdy backbone of Wales.

Builth Wells

The town grew up beneath the walls of a castle built by the Normans in 1098, a stronghold that changed hands many times in the conflicts with the Welsh. Only the motte, the earthworks, of this castle survive. Builth is important as the centre of a remote district largely devoted to agriculture and the Old Courtroom provides a cultural venue with its arts centre and cinema.

On the outskirts of the town a memorial commemorates Prince Llewellyn, last Welsh-born Prince of Wales, who was killed nearby in battle with the English in 1282. Also on the outskirts is the showground where the Royal Welsh Show is held each year – the main event of the farming calendar in Wales and the borders.

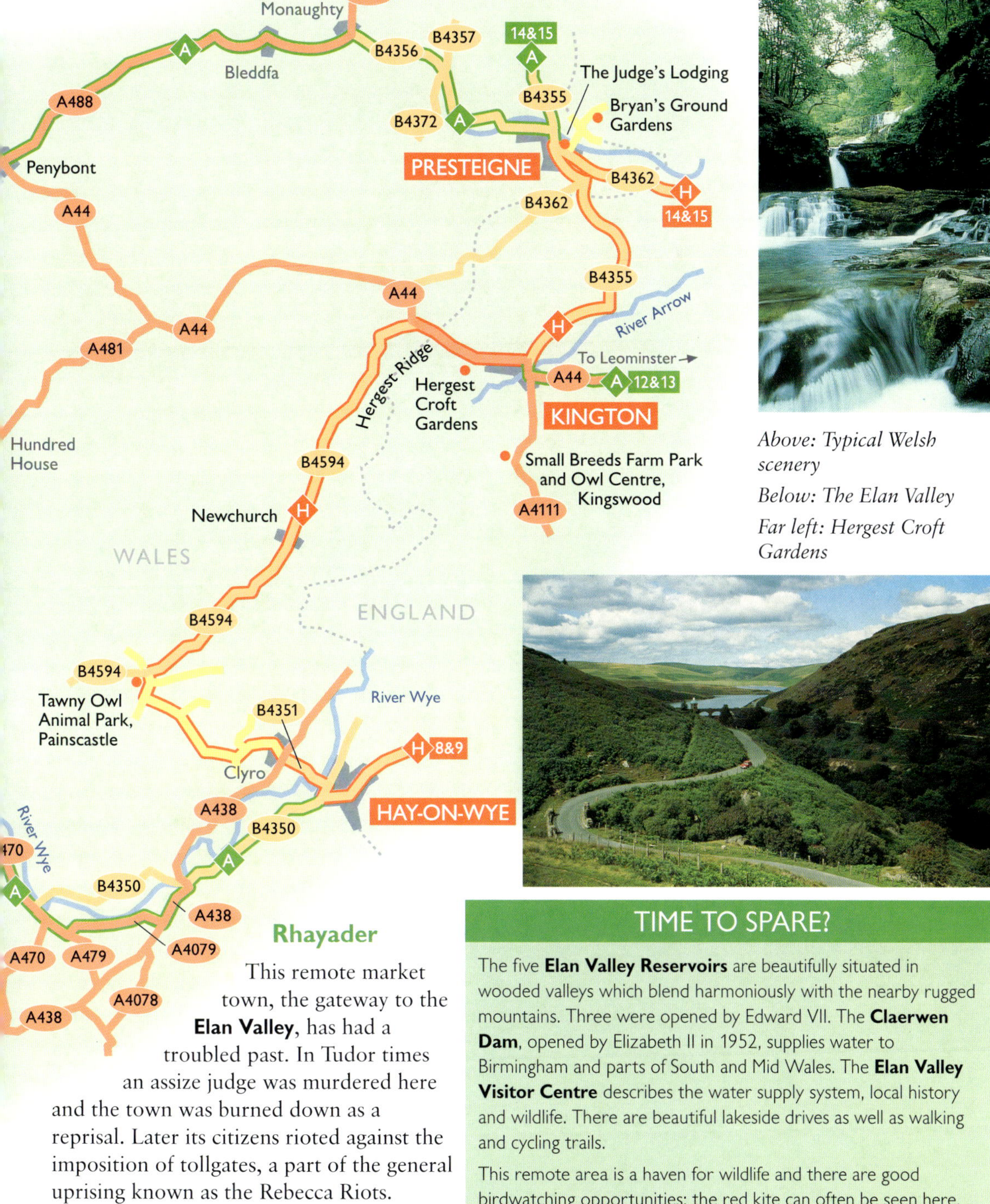

Above: Typical Welsh scenery

Below: The Elan Valley

Far left: Hergest Croft Gardens

Rhayader

This remote market town, the gateway to the **Elan Valley**, has had a troubled past. In Tudor times an assize judge was murdered here and the town was burned down as a reprisal. Later its citizens rioted against the imposition of tollgates, a part of the general uprising known as the Rebecca Riots. Prince Llewellyn was laid to rest at nearby Abbey-cwm-hir after his death in battle at Builth Wells. Welsh masters of fire and glass can be seen at work at **Welsh Royal Crystal**. A guided tour shows how crystal glass is made, from the initial blowing to the final cutting and polishing.

TIME TO SPARE?

The five **Elan Valley Reservoirs** are beautifully situated in wooded valleys which blend harmoniously with the nearby rugged mountains. Three were opened by Edward VII. The **Claerwen Dam**, opened by Elizabeth II in 1952, supplies water to Birmingham and parts of South and Mid Wales. The **Elan Valley Visitor Centre** describes the water supply system, local history and wildlife. There are beautiful lakeside drives as well as walking and cycling trails.

This remote area is a haven for wildlife and there are good birdwatching opportunities; the red kite can often be seen here.

No sound is here
Save the stream that shrills
And now and then
A cry of faint wailing, when the kite
Comes sailing o'er the crags
Or struggling lamb bleats for its mother.

Rev. William Bowles

Alternative route to Leominster

This follows a lovely section of the **Black and White Village Trail**, passing through countryside where 'past and present blend in a timeless tapestry'. Here you can visit churches, pubs or village shops to find a flavour of the essential England.

Pembridge church has an interesting belltower – it stands separate from the church in a corner of the churchyard. Also at Pembridge, **Dunkerton's Cider Mill and Restaurant** is interesting, offering the chance to view the cider mill and sample the produce with a meal! Other historic buildings in these villages include a unique eighteenth-century dovecote at **Eardisland**, now a visitor centre, and **Burton Court**, built in the fourteenth century, which houses an extensive collection of European and Oriental costumes.

Leominster

The town was already flourishing in the seventh century but may have got its name (pronounced 'Lemster') four hundred years later, from the Saxon Earl Leofric who caused his wife, Lady Godiva, to make her famous ride through Coventry.

Leominster has a wealth of timber-framed buildings dating from Tudor and Jacobean times, quite a few of them occupied by antique dealers. Oak trees were once known as 'the weed of Herefordshire', which is why so many houses here were built of timber and such fine examples remain today. The more lavishly carved the timber framing, the wealthier the occupants! One of the best of them is Grange Court, built in 1633 as the market house but moved to its present position in the nineteenth century. There is also the **Priory Church**, which houses a ducking stool, used as late as 1809 to silence over-talkative women!

Garden lovers will enjoy the Van Kampen Gardens at **Hampton Court**, Hope-under-Dinmore, with its maze, wisteria arch, and a conservatory designed by Joseph Paxton.

Lord Coningsby lived here in the eighteenth century – the last nobleman in England to employ a jester in his household.

Far left, top: Leominster Priory

Far left, bottom: Pembridge belltower

Above: Burton Court

Left: Dunkerton's Cider Mill

Below: Cricket at Leominster

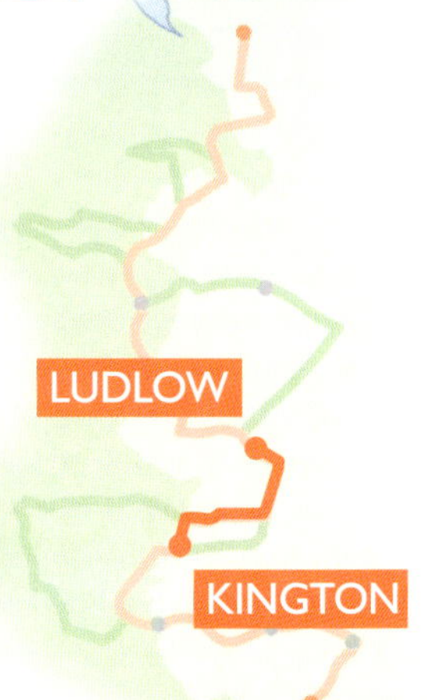

Kington

This Herefordshire market town probably takes its name from King Edward the Confessor who seized it from the Princes of Brecknock in 1055. It is a delightful little place, with a relaxed but not sleepy atmosphere, and is an excellent base for walkers who have the opportunity to sample lengths of the Offa's Dyke Path or the Mortimer Trail as both run through Kington. It is home to England's highest golf course. There is also a town museum and a fine parish church, **St Mary's**, which dates from the twelfth century.

The **Kingswood Small Breeds Farm Park and Owl Centre** is on the outskirts of the town.

Presteigne

A charming old Welsh town with many black and white buildings, Presteigne stands on the banks of the River Lugg amongst splendid scenery. Its position just on the English side of Offa's Dyke gives it its character and a turbulent history. As George Borrow wrote in

1867, it is a town 'neither in Wales nor in England but simply in Radnorshire'.

The Judge's Lodging at the Shire Hall has been painstakingly restored in keeping with the period of its heyday. Visitors see the courtroom and cells as well as the gloomy gas-lit servants' quarters.

The village of **Shobdon** is in England and is famous for its church, built for the second Viscount Bateman in 1756. The architect was Horace Walpole who chose the picturesque 'Strawberry Hill' Gothic style for which he is renowned. There is an attractive eighteenth-century watermill at **Mortimer's Cross** cared for by English Heritage. The place takes its name from being the battlefield where a decisive battle of the Wars of the Roses took

place in 1461 which ensured the succession to the throne of the Yorkist Edward IV, a descendant of the Mortimers.

Croft Castle, a National Trust property, is a Norman border castle which has evolved into a stately home over the centuries. **Berrington Hall** (also NT) was built 1778–83 to the designs of Henry Holland, and is a mansion with elegant décor and furnishings and fabulous formal gardens.

16&17 H
A49
River Corve
A4113
Bromfield
A4117
River Teme
LUDLOW
Ludlow Castle
Offa's Dyke Visitor Centre
B4355
A488
River Teme
A4113
Knighton
A488
B4355
B4361
Richards Castle
A49
River Teme
H
B4362
A
10&11
B4356
B4357
T
ENGLAND
WALES
The Judge's Lodging
Wigmore Castle (EH)
A4110
Croft Castle (NT)
B4355
Bryan's Ground Gardens
B4372
Berrington Hall (NT)
B4362
River Lugg
PRESTEIGNE
B4362
B4361
Mortimer's Cross Water Mill & Battle Centre (EH)
B4362
H
A
12&13
To Leominster
To Leominster
Shobdon Church and Arches
B4355
10&11
H
KINGTON
Hergest Croft Gardens
A44
A 12&13
A4111
Small Breeds Farm Park and Owl Centre, Kingswood

TIME TO SPARE?

Knighton – Welsh name *Trefyclo* – sits beside the fast-flowing River Teme on the border with Shropshire. Its picturesque narrow streets boast many fascinating antique shops.

Offa's Dyke runs through the town. The Dyke was built by Offa, King of Mercia (757–796), in the eighth century as a boundary between Mercia and the Welsh kingdoms to prevent cross-border raids. It utilises a combination of rivers, artificial banks and ditches and stretches for 100 miles (160km), from the mouth of the River Wye to the estuary of the Dee, making it the most extensive linear earthwork in Britain. In places it is still six feet (2m) high. You can find out more about it at the **Offa's Dyke Visitor Centre**.

Far left: Presteigne
Left: Croft Castle (NT)
Above left: Kington
Top: Berrington Hall (NT)

'Or come you home of Monday when Ludlow market hums...'
A.E. Housman, *A Shropshire Lad*

'I never expect to sleep again in a place so beautiful.'
Shropshire and A.E. Housman, Willa Catha.

Rugged wilderness and rich farmland, ancient villages and hamlets, hidden valleys overlooked by hillside pastures; South Shropshire offers a landscape of continual surprises and great beauty.

Ludlow

Encircled by the rivers Corve and Teme, the medieval town of Ludlow breathes history at every turn. Acclaimed by John Betjeman as the loveliest town in England, Ludlow has nearly 500 listed buildings, many of them standing on streets which were laid out when the castle was built. Ludlow also has more than its share of Georgian town houses, reflecting its popularity with prosperous county families in the eighteenth century. Modern Ludlow is a thriving market town celebrated for its excellent restaurants – some of them mentioned in the Michelin guide.

TIME TO SPARE?

Bury Ditches Hill Fort is one of the most formidable Iron Age forts in South Shropshire, with all-embracing views. It dates from the first century BC.

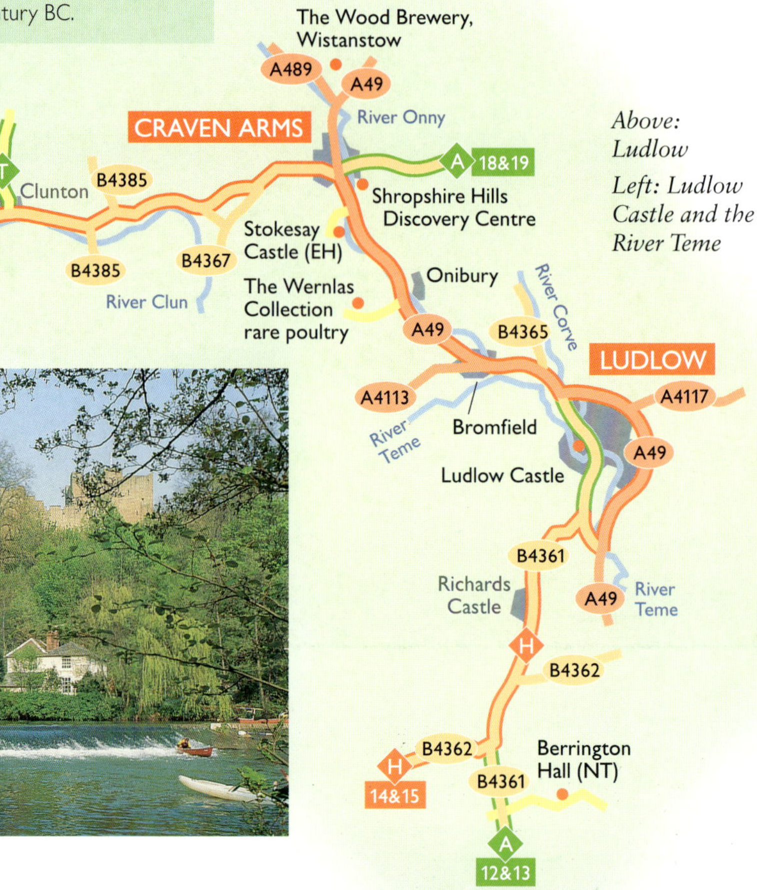

The Wood Brewery, Wistanstow
A489
A49
River Onny
22&23 H
Bury Ditches
A488
CRAVEN ARMS
A 18&19
T
Clunton
B4385
B4368
Shropshire Hills Discovery Centre
B4368
Castle (EH)
CLUN
A488
B4385
B4367
Stokesay Castle (EH)
River Clun
The Wernlas Collection rare poultry
Onibury
River Corve
A49
B4365
LUDLOW
A4113
A4117
Bromfield
River Teme
Ludlow Castle
A49
B4361
Richards Castle
A49
River Teme
H
B4362
B4362
H 14&15
Berrington Hall (NT)
B4361
A 12&13

Above: Ludlow

Left: Ludlow Castle and the River Teme

Visitor Questionnaire

We would be grateful if you could spare a few minutes to answer the following questions. Your answers will help us to improve the information and services we offer to visitors.

Your questionnaire will be entered into a **PRIZE DRAW** (drawn at the end of each year) and three winners will receive a bottle of excellent Tanners Champagne.

1 **Where did you first hear about the Hidden Highway?**

____

2 **Which part of the route did you drive?**

From ______________________________

To ______________________________

3 **In which month(s) of the year was your trip?**

____

4 **How long have you spent travelling along the Hidden Highway?**

1 day ◯

2 days ◯

3 days ◯

more ◯ (please state) ______________

5 **How many people were there in your party?**______________

6 **Where did you stay?** ______________

____

____

____

____

____

7 **How did you book your accommodation?**

Telephoned accommodation direct ◯

Called in en route at an accommodation ◯

Through:

- a web site – please give address ____________________
- a Tourist Information Centre at ____________________
- Herefordshire & Wye Valley brochure ◯
- the Shropshire brochure ◯
- the Brilliant Breaks booking line ◯

Other ____

8 **How would you rate the Hidden Highway guide?**

Route instructions

Excellent ◯ Good ◯ Fair ◯ Poor ◯ Very poor ◯

Readability

Excellent ◯ Good ◯ Fair ◯ Poor ◯ Very poor ◯

9 **How did you enjoy the experience of the Hidden Highway route?**

Level of interest

Excellent ◯ Good ◯ Fair ◯ Poor ◯ Very poor ◯

Overall enjoyment

Excellent ◯ Good ◯ Fair ◯ Poor ◯ Very poor ◯

10 **Have you visited any attractions (castles, gardens, museums etc) along the Hidden Highway?**

Yes ◯ No ◯

If yes please state which one(s) ______________________

____

____

____

11 **Have you driven any of the route on a previous visit?**

Yes ◯ No ◯ Not sure ◯

Would you like to receive further information on:

Herefordshire ◯ Shropshire ◯ Mid Wales ◯

Name ______________________

Address ______________________

____

____

____

Thank you for your time

Please return this form in a sealed envelope to:

Shropshire Tourism
FREEPOST NWW 4092A
Shrewsbury
SY1 3ZA

There is no need to add a stamp

The **Ludlow Marches Food and Drink Festival** is an annual event held in September.

Perched on a cliff above the River Teme, **Ludlow Castle** has dominated its town and the surrounding countryside for 900 years. The original Norman stronghold was transformed into a medieval palace by Roger Mortimer, the most powerful of all Marcher lords. Later it became a royal palace and was the headquarters of the Council of the Marches which governed Wales and five English counties. It was the home of the two young princes, sons of Edward IV, who died so tragically in the Tower of London, and of Henry VII's son, Prince Arthur, who brought his bride Catherine of Aragon here. The castle's atmospheric grounds host Ludlow's annual festival which features a major Shakespearean production and runs for two weeks in June and July.

St Laurence's is one of the six largest parish churches in the country. The top of its 132-foot (40m) tower is reached by 202 steps and there are beautifully carved misericords. A.E. Housman's ashes are buried near the north door.

The timber-framed **Feathers Hotel** was the town house of a lawyer in 1619 and first became an inn c.1670. The wonderful carving on its black and white façade can only be described as 'exuberant'.

Collectors will enjoy Ludlow's numerous antique shops, bookshops and galleries, as well as the antique and other colourful markets held in the square from March to Christmas.

Stokesay Castle (EH), with its half-timbered gatehouse and the church close by, makes a favourite subject for photographers and artists. This fairytale thirteenth-century fortified manor house is the finest and most perfectly preserved of its kind in the UK.

Housed within a unique grass-roofed building, **Secret Hills – The Shropshire Hills Discovery Centre** invites you to experience the heritage and culture of this Area of Outstanding Natural Beauty. A simulated balloon flight reveals the magic of the countryside – the 'blue remembered hills' immortalised by A.E. Housman in *A Shropshire Lad*.

Above: The Feathers Hotel, Ludlow
Below: Stokesay Castle (EH)

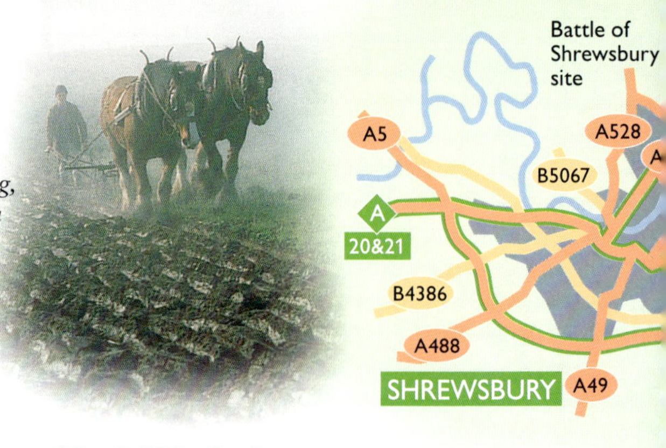

Right: At Acton Scott Historic Working Farm, experience nineteenth-century farm life, from butter-making to threshing, and enjoy demonstrations from the wheelwright, farrier and blacksmith

This part of the route takes you through Corvedale, a beautiful valley overlooked by the undulating Clee Hills. Along the way you will find peaceful villages, ancient churches and traditional inns. Dick Turpin is said to have stayed at the Swan Inn at Aston Munslow.

Shipton Hall is an impressive mansion built in 1587. The parish church here has a plaque commemorating four local children who were sent to America on the Mayflower.

Wenlock Edge

The sixteen-mile (26km) escarpment began life as a coral reef south of the Equator many millions of years ago. Now in the care of the National Trust, its limestone woodland is a haven for wildlife.

The Edge is well known for its ghosts. 'Major's Leap' takes its name from the spot where Major Smallman, desperate to escape pursuing Roundheads, made his horse jump over the edge. He survived but his mount died and his ghost haunts the place.

There are literary connections here too, not just with Housman but also with Mary Webb, author of *Precious Bane* and *Gone to Earth*, who used to ride with her father along the Edge in a pony and trap.

On Wenlock Edge the wood's in trouble;
His forest fleece the Wrekin heaves;
A.E. Housman

Much Wenlock

Much Wenlock is a charming medieval market town. The picturesque ruins of Wenlock Priory are the remains of a Cluniac monastery built on the site of the original Abbey of St Milburgha, founded in 680.

The town also has a half-timbered **guildhall** dating from the sixteenth century, a **parish church** with impressive Norman nave and chancel, and the Much Wenlock Museum.

In 1850 Dr William Penny Brookes founded the Wenlock Olympian Games which were the inspiration for the modern Olympics. Much Wenlock still stages Olympian Games each July.

Buildwas Abbey is a ruined Cistercian monastery set in wooded countryside to the west of Ironbridge. It is cared for by English Heritage.

B4370
The Wood Brewery, Wistanstow
Acton Scott Historic Working Farm
Aston Munslo
A489
A49
CRAVEN ARMS
River Onny
A
B4367
B4368
B4365
22&23 H
Shropshire Hills Discovery Centre
Stokesay Castle (EH)
A49
Onibury
The Wernlas Collection rare poultry
H
16&17

Below: View from Wenlock Edge

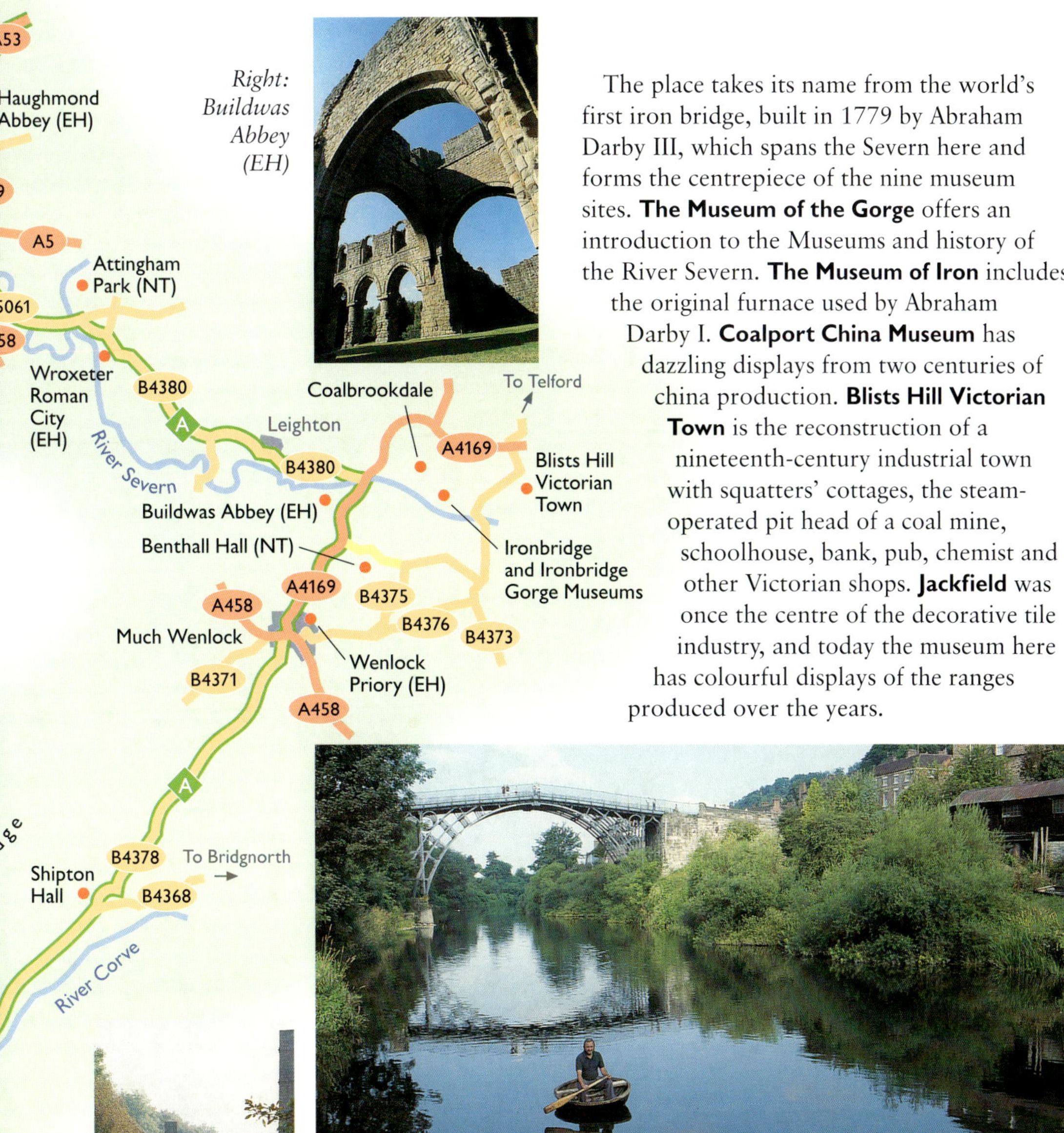

Right: Buildwas Abbey (EH)

The place takes its name from the world's first iron bridge, built in 1779 by Abraham Darby III, which spans the Severn here and forms the centrepiece of the nine museum sites. **The Museum of the Gorge** offers an introduction to the Museums and history of the River Severn. **The Museum of Iron** includes the original furnace used by Abraham Darby I. **Coalport China Museum** has dazzling displays from two centuries of china production. **Blists Hill Victorian Town** is the reconstruction of a nineteenth-century industrial town with squatters' cottages, the steam-operated pit head of a coal mine, schoolhouse, bank, pub, chemist and other Victorian shops. **Jackfield** was once the centre of the decorative tile industry, and today the museum here has colourful displays of the ranges produced over the years.

Ironbridge

The award-winning **Ironbridge Gorge Museums** are set within the deep wooded gorge of the River Severn which is a designated World Heritage Site. This spectacular and beautiful area offers the visitor a unique chance to step back in time and explore the birthplace of the Industrial Revolution. This dates from 1709 when Abraham Darby I perfected the mass production of cast iron.

Wroxeter Roman City was the fourth largest city in Roman Britain in the second century. Today visitors see the impressive remains of the municipal baths which include the tallest surviving Roman masonry to be seen in this country. Treasures unearthed in the excavations are displayed in the on-site museum. Adjacent is **Wroxeter Roman Vineyard**, which produces excellent wines with crisp English character.

Above: The Iron Bridge (EH)
Left: Blists Hill Victorian Town

Shrewsbury

Shropshire's county town occupies a loop in the River Severn, a site chosen by its medieval builders since it was easily defendable. Shrewsbury is perhaps England's finest Tudor town, with numerous black and white buildings on cobbled streets, hidden 'shuts' and passages with ancient names often reflecting the trades once plied there; Fish Street, Milk Street and Grope Lane (a former 'red light' area!). Shrewsbury is a fine town for shopping – everything from second-hand books to antiques and art deco – and walking. A guided walk or following the town trail from the Tourist Information Centre will help you discover more about Shrewsbury's exciting history and you can even follow a **Brother Cadfael Trail** and see the places mentioned in Ellis Peters' famous mysteries.

Find out even more about the fictional monk by visiting **The Shrewsbury Quest** where you can experience the sights, sounds and smells of the twelfth-century town and learn about life in a monastery. Opposite The Quest is **Shrewsbury Abbey**, founded in 1083 and at the heart of the Cadfael tales.

Shrewsbury is known as the Town of Flowers and holds the famous **Shrewsbury Flower Show** every August.

The town's most famous son is Charles Darwin, whose theory of evolution shocked the world. Wilfred Owen (1893–1918), arguably the greatest of all war poets, spent childhood and adolescence here,

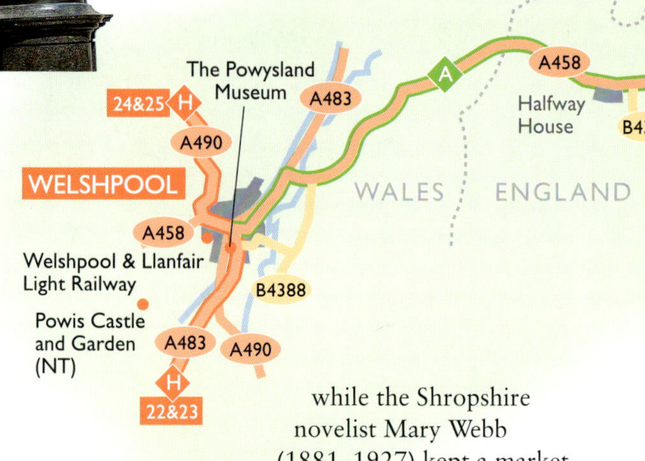

while the Shropshire novelist Mary Webb (1881–1927) kept a market stall here and disguised Shrewsbury as 'Silverton' in her books, which include *Precious Bane* and *Gone to Earth*.

Standing proudly on its hill, **Shrewsbury Castle** dates from the 1160s. It is now home to the **Shropshire Regimental Museum**.

Centre: Charles Darwin statue

Top and left: Shrewsbury

Attingham Park (NT) is a splendid neo-classical mansion which embodies country life on a grand scale. Enjoy the splendid Regency interiors with magnificently furnished state rooms. The house is set in sweeping riverside parkland laid out by Humphry Repton.

Rowley's House Museum is a beautiful half-timbered mansion where you will find collections and galleries interpreting the rich history of Shropshire and its county town. **Mythstories** traces the origins of myths and legends across the centuries.

Just to the north of the town, **Battlefield** was the site of the Battle of Shrewsbury in 1403 when Henry IV defeated Harry Hotspur.

Top left: Haughmond Abbey (EH)
Above: Attingham Park (NT)

Left: Hodnet Hall Gardens

TIME TO SPARE?

Hodnet Hall has sixty acres (24 ha) of magnificent gardens, with formal beds and colourful shrubs, a chain of ornamental lakes and a tearoom where hunting trophies are displayed.

Hawkstone Historic Park and Follies is the most spectacular man-made landscape in Europe and a fine place for exploration and admiration with its caves, cliffs, grottoes, tunnels and Red Castle. It was the location for some of the filming of the Narnia chronicles of C.S. Lewis.

The rugged beauty of the Long Mynd and Stiperstones makes for a wild and mysterious borderland, which has been farmed and fought over for centuries.

Clun

'Clunton and Clunbury,
Clungunford and Clun
Are the quietest places
Under the sun'

A Shropshire Lad,
A.E. Housman

There are excellent shops, many devoted to books and antiques. Two inns produce and sell real ale, The Six Bells and the Three Tuns where you will also find the **Hobbs Museum of Beer and Brewing**.

Other attractions include the **House on Crutches**, a delightful sixteenth century house which is now a museum of local history, and the **Railway and Transport Museum**.

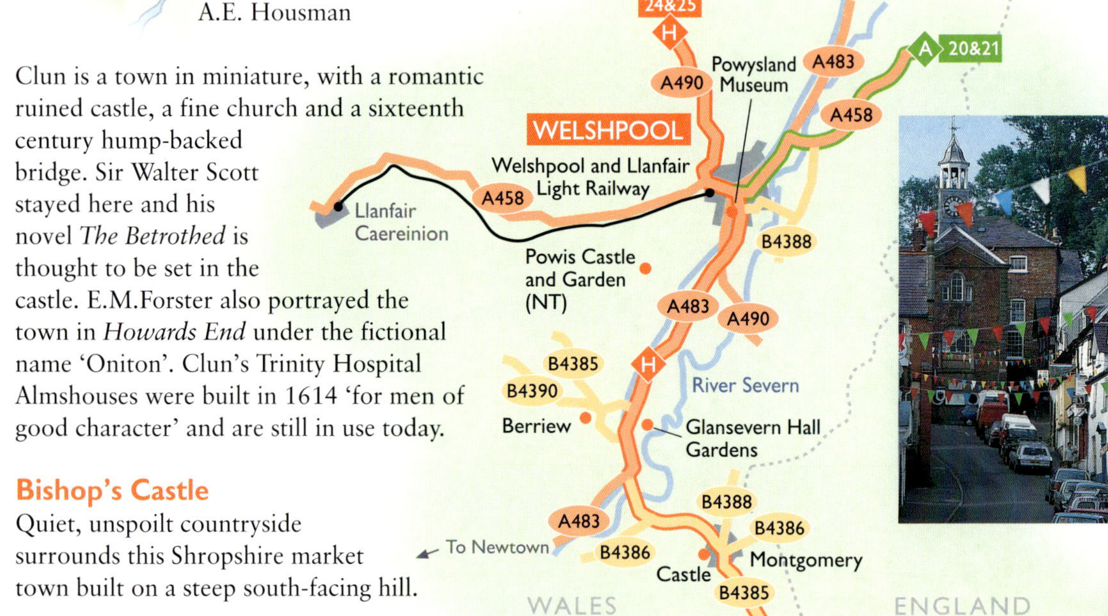

Clun is a town in miniature, with a romantic ruined castle, a fine church and a sixteenth century hump-backed bridge. Sir Walter Scott stayed here and his novel *The Betrothed* is thought to be set in the castle. E.M.Forster also portrayed the town in *Howards End* under the fictional name 'Oniton'. Clun's Trinity Hospital Almshouses were built in 1614 'for men of good character' and are still in use today.

Bishop's Castle

Quiet, unspoilt countryside surrounds this Shropshire market town built on a steep south-facing hill.

Above: Bishop's Castle

Left: Clun Castle (EH)

Facing page top: Powis Castle (NT)

Facing page centre: Welshpool

Facing page bottom: Welshpool and Llanfair Light Railway

Montgomery

The town of Montgomery lies at the foot of a precipitous outcrop on the summit of which Henry III built an impregnable castle which commanded one of the few crossings over the River Severn into Mid Wales. Its strategic importance led to it being besieged many times. Today romantic ruins look out over spectacular views. Montgomery town is a conservation area with many fine Georgian buildings.

The poet John Donne wrote his famous lines on a primrose when at Montgomery in 1625, and the flower's successors still carpet the ground hereabouts in Spring.

Places to visit include the **Old Bell Museum and Exhibition Centre**, housed in a sixteenth-century building. The **Robber's Grave** is the resting place of John Davies who was hanged in 1821. Protesting against the sentence, he predicted that if he was innocent no grass would grow on his grave for 100 years – apparently, none did!

Glansevern Hall Gardens are the eighteen-acre (7 ha) grounds of a hall built in Greek revival style. There is a lakeside walk, rose, rock and water gardens, unusual trees, plus a tearoom and garden shop.

Berriew is a picturesque village with fine examples of the black and white half-timbered cottages common to this area. Perhaps surprisingly, the village is home to the avant garde **Andrew Logan Gallery** and the showrooms for the popular **Silver Scenes** jewellery.

Medieval **Powis Castle** (NT) is perhaps the most romantic of all British castles, originally built in the fourteenth century as a fortress for Welsh Princes. Today it contains the finest collections of paintings and furniture in Wales, including a beautiful hoard of treasures brought back from India by Lord Clive, including jade, ivory, and bronze items. Don't miss the world-famous hanging gardens with their enormous yew trees, colourful borders and statues.

Welshpool

The ancient county town of Montgomeryshire, Welshpool has its share of attractive historic buildings. Outstanding amongst these are **The Buttery and Prentice Traders' buildings** with their delicately carved timber fronts, and the hexagonal **Cock Pit** which was used until 1849 when the 'sport' was made illegal.

The Powysland Museum, housed in the Old Shropshire Union Canal warehouse, gives a fascinating insight into the history of Montgomeryshire.

Canal boat trips along the Montgomery Canal are available from the wharf between April and November. From Raven Square, gleaming **steam trains** run by local enthusiasts carry passengers through rolling hills to Llanfair Caereinion.

Left: Oswestry market

Oswestry

The name of the town comes from Oswald, the Christian king of Northumbria, who was defeated by the pagan Prince Penda of Mercia in 642 and torn limb from limb. His remains were nailed to a tree – hence Oswald's Tree, Oswestry.

Today it is a bustling market town with a rare character gleaned from centuries of history. Its excellent shopping centre serves a wide surrounding area as does its weekly market, given its charter in 1190, which, with over 100 stalls, is the largest market in the Welsh borders.

The Reverend W.D. Spooner was educated at Oswestry Grammar School, now the **Heritage Centre**. His famous mis-sayings include 'shoving leopard' and 'let me sew you into a sheet'!

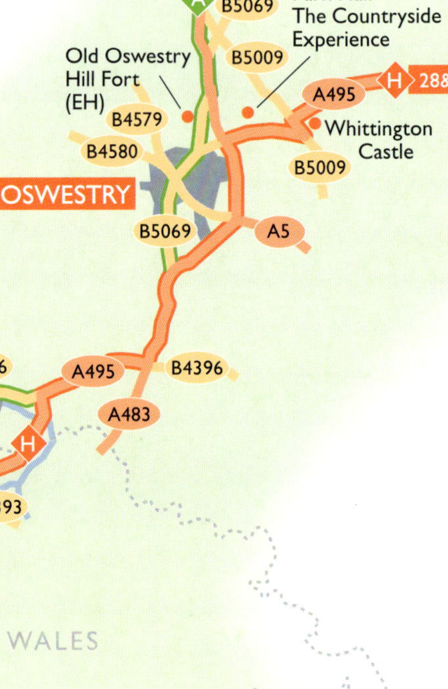

Wilfred Owen, the most famous of war poets, was born in Oswestry in 1893.

The town is a mecca for hot air ballooning enthusiasts. Per Lindstrand's firm is based here and has made balloons for Richard Branson.

Old Oswestry Hill Fort (EH) is a large Iron Age fort with a succession of ramparts which covers 68 acres (27.5ha). Its Welsh name, Caer Gogyrfan, links it to the legendary father of Queen Guinevere, and she is supposed to have been born here.

Why not visit **Oswestry Transport Museum** and **Park Hall – The Countryside Experience**; the latter is a restored Victorian farm with rare breeds and grand shire horses.

Just the twin-towered gatehouse remains of **Whittington Castle** but it is an impressive and picturesque sight, standing beside its moat. The castle is steeped in history. During the 1200s it was the home of Fulk Fitz Warine who is reputed to have won the castle and the hand of Lady Mellet in a tournament, her ladyship having vowed that she would only marry a brave knight.

Left: Ballooning
Above: Old Oswestry Hill Fort (EH)
Below: Whittington Castle

TIME TO SPARE?

Llanrhaeadr-Ym-Mochnant is a delightful little place whose chief claim to fame is that it is where Bishop Morgan completed the first translation of the Bible into Welsh. More recently it was the location for the film The *Englishman Who Went Up A Hill And Came Down A Mountain*, starring Hugh Grant.

In the mountains beyond Llanrhaeadr-Ym-Mochnant you will find one of the seven wonders of Wales: **Pistyll Rhaeadr Waterfall**, at 240 feet (73m) the highest in England and Wales and 60 feet (18m) higher than Niagara Falls. George Borrow described it in *Wild Wales* as 'an immense skein of silk agitated and disturbed by tempestuous blasts .... I never saw water falling so gracefully.'

This part of the route travels deep into the Berwyn Mountains and offers stunning views – some of the roads are very narrow.

Llanfyllin

This old market town on the upper reaches of the River Cain takes its name from Myllin, a Celtic saint of the seventh century who was the first cleric to baptise using total immersion. The restored holy well bearing his name, above the town, provides great views.

Llangedwyn Mill and Craft Workshops form an attractive group of stone buildings on the riverbank converted into workshops for a silversmith, a potter, and a stained glass worker.

Lake Vyrnwy

Here the mountains embrace a lake containing some twelve billion gallons (54bn litres) of water resulting in scenery reminiscent of the Alps.

Top: Pistyll Rhaeadr

Left: Lake Vyrnwy

Surprisingly, this apparently natural beauty was created by Liverpool Corporation to give a water supply to the city, some seventy-five miles (120km) from here. **The Lake Vyrnwy Visitor Centre** provides information on the area including birdwatching, lakeside walking, cycling and driving trails.

Above and right: Lake Vyrnwy

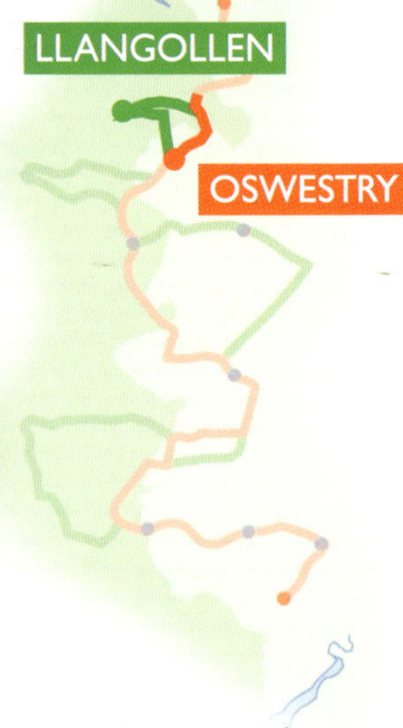

A nineteenth-century rhyme places six of the 'Seven Wonders of Wales' in the North Wales borderlands:

Pistyll Rhaeadr and Wrexham Steeple,
Snowdon's Mountain without its people,
Overton Yew Trees, St Winifride's Well,
Llangollen Bridge and Gresford Bells...

Chirk Castle (NT)

The magnificent castle has been continuously inhabited since its construction in the thirteenth century. It guards the beautiful Ceiriog valley and its elegant staterooms contrast with the miserable dungeons. There is a picturesque hawkhouse in the lovely gardens.

Chirk Aqueduct was built by the famous engineer, Thomas Telford. Seventy feet (21m) high, it spans the Ceiriog valley with ten striding arches. Even higher at 126 feet (38m) is the **Pontcysyllte Aqueduct** which carries the Llangollen Canal over the River Dee. You can walk across or take a forty-five-minute voyage on a canal boat – either way it is an unforgettable experience. The Shropshire Union and Llangollen Canals criss-cross the area, and pleasure boats offer trips on them from several locations.

Llangollen

This beautiful town is famed for its steam railway, canal, and the annual **Eisteddfod International Music Festival**, which attracts participants from more than thirty nations. The fourteenth-century bridge is one of the 'Seven Wonders of Wales'.

Celebrated local characters include 'The Ladies of Llangollen', who lived at **Plas Newydd** with their maid, 'Molly the Basher'. The Ladies were two Irish women who eloped here from Waterford and entertained many national and literary figures of their day, including the Duke of Wellington, William Wordsworth and Sir Walter Scott. Plas Newydd is an elegant black and white house where the classical style is mixed with Gothic with picturesque results. The interior has a large painting by Rex Whistler, an artist who had associations with Plas Newydd in the 1930s.

The **BBC Doctor Who Exhibition** at Llangollen is a favourite attraction with adults and children alike.

The **Llangollen Railway** is a standard-gauge steam railway which winds through the beautiful Dee Valley for several miles to a terminus at Carrog.

The ruins of **Valle Crucis Abbey** are just two miles (3.2km) from Llangollen. This is the most interesting ecclesiastical ruin in North Wales. Much of the west front of the abbey church survives, including the rose window.

Top: The Llangollen Canal crossing the Chirk Aqueduct
Above: Llangollen Bridge
Left: Valle Crucis

Ellesmere

The town takes its name from Ellesmere, the largest of six glacial lakes which make up 'Shropshire's Lake District'. The pretty market town has a medieval street plan lined by timber-framed buildings as well as some elegant Georgian houses. Visit the **Meres Visitor Centre** to pick up information about the town and its meres, including leaflets on walks and bird watching.

Canal Wharf, where colourful pleasure craft have their moorings, is a reminder that Ellesmere was once the centre of a busy canal network. Thomas Telford drew his plans for the Llangollen Canal from his offices at Ellesmere.

A circular crown bowling green on the site of the Norman motte and bailey castle is reputedly the oldest bowling green of this type in the country.

At nearby **Erbistock** on an idyllic spot by the River Dee stands St Hilary's, a small sandstone church on ground hallowed by more than 1000 years of worship.

Overton is home to a group of tall yew trees that has been growing here since medieval times, another of the 'Seven Wonders of Wales'.

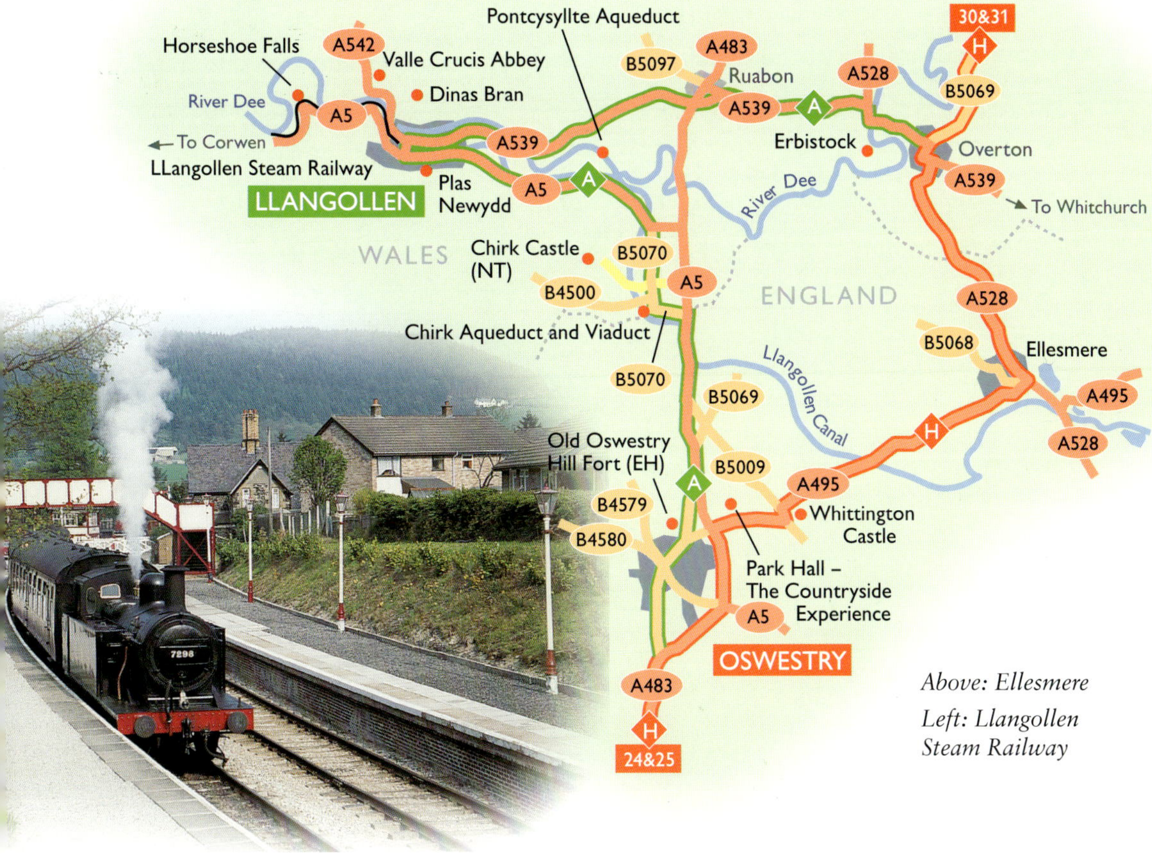

Horseshoe Falls
River Dee
A542
Valle Crucis Abbey
Dinas Bran
Pontcysyllte Aqueduct
A5
← To Corwen
LLangollen Steam Railway
LLANGOLLEN
A539
Plas Newydd
B5097
A483
Ruabon
A539
A528
B5069
30&31
Erbistock
Overton
A539
To Whitchurch
River Dee
WALES
Chirk Castle (NT)
B5070
B4500
A5
ENGLAND
Chirk Aqueduct and Viaduct
B5070
A528
B5068
Ellesmere
Llangollen Canal
B5069
A495
A528
Old Oswestry Hill Fort (EH)
B5009
A495
B4579
Whittington Castle
B4580
Park Hall – The Countryside Experience
A5
OSWESTRY
A483
24&25

Above: Ellesmere

Left: Llangollen Steam Railway

As you drive through rural Cheshire you will pass through villages of traditional black and white buildings where time seems to have stood still. Cattle graze in the lush meadows and wild flowers flourish on the verges. Some village names recall Anglo-Saxon settlements while others, like Aldford and Malpas, were recorded in the Domesday Book.

William the Conqueror built a chain of motte-and-bailey castles from North Cheshire to **Malpas**, where an eighteenth-century market place survives. A local saying goes 'Malpas ales and Malpas gales, cheer the farmer, fill his pails'.

Farndon, a village in an area that witnessed many cross-border conflicts over the years, has a medieval sandstone bridge linking England with Wales. It is supposed to be haunted by the screaming ghosts of two sons of Prince Madog. The boys were drowned here by their guardians.

Aldford is an excellent example of a nineteenth-century estate village, one of five villages on the Grosvenor estate. Its cottages have low pitched roofs and bear distinctive diamond patterns. The nearby village of Dodleston was the base for Oliver Cromwell's troops during the Siege of Chester in the Civil War. Across the bridge in **Holt**, St Chad's church shows bullet holes from Civil War muskets. A Roman outpost here made tiles and pottery for their fortress at Deva in Chester.

Chester

The county town of Cheshire is one of Britain's showpieces of history and architecture. Its heritage extends back 2000 years to the Roman Invasion when Chester had the name 'Deva' and it became the headquarters of the famous Twentieth Legion of the Roman army. They girdled the city with a wall that survives today as the most complete city wall

Top: Chester city centre
Above: Chester
Left: Chester cathedral

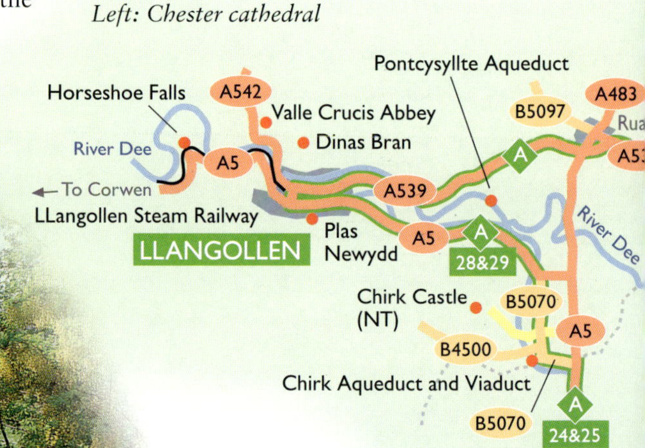